Principles of Bookkeeping [Controls]

AAT Level 2 Certificate in Accounting

© Michael Fardon, Debbie Board, 2022.

All rights reserved. No part of this publication may be reproduced, stored in a retrieval system, or transmitted in any form or by any means, electronic, mechanical, photo-copying, recording or otherwise, without the prior consent of the copyright owners, or in accordance with the provisions of the Copyright, Designs and Patents Act 1988, or under the terms of any licence permitting limited copying issued by the Copyright Licensing Agency, Saffron House, 6-10 Kirby Street, London EC1N 8TS.

Image of owl © Eric Isselée-Fotolia.com

Published by Osborne Books Limited, Printed and bound by Stroma Ltd, UK.

Email books@osbornebooks.co.uk, Website www.osbornebooks.co.uk

ISBN 978-1-911198-85-7

how to use this Wise Guide

This Wise Guide has been designed to supplement your Tutorial and Workbook. It has two main aims:

- to reinforce your learning as you study your course
- to help you prepare for your online assessment

This Wise Guide is organised in the specific topic areas listed on pages 4 and 5. These individual topic areas have been designed to cover the main areas of study, concentrating on specific areas of difficulty. There is also an index at the back to help you find the areas you are studying or revising.

The Owl symbolises wisdom, and acts as your tutor, introducing and explaining topics. Please let us know if he is doing his job properly. If you have feedback on this material please email books@osbornebooks.co.uk.

Thank you and good luck with your study and revision.

Osborne Books

REVISION TIPS

*'**OWL**' stands for: **O**bserve **W**rite **L**earn*

There are a number of well-known ways in which you can remember information:

- *You can remember what it looks like on the page. Diagrams, lists, mind-maps, colour coding for different types of information, all help you **observe** and remember.*

- *You can remember what you **write** down. Flash cards, post-it notes around the bathroom mirror, notes on a mobile phone all help. It is the process of writing which fixes the information in the brain.*

- *You can **learn** by using this Wise Guide. Read through each topic carefully and then prepare your own written version on flash cards, post-it notes, wall charts – anything that you can see regularly.*

- *Lastly, give yourself **chill out** time, your brain a chance to recover and the information time to sink in. Promise yourself treats when you have finished studying – a drink, chocolate, a work out. Relax! And pass.*

list of contents

1	Payment methods	6
2	Payment methods and the bank balance	12
3	Bank reconciliation statement	16
4	Receivables Ledger control account	26
5	Payables Ledger control account	34
6	VAT control account	40
7	Journals – introduction	44
8	Journals – opening entries	48
9	Journals – irrecoverable debts	52
10	Journals – payroll transactions	54

11	Extracting an initial Trial Balance	62
12	Journals – correction of errors and suspense account	68
13	Redrafting the Trial Balance	76
14	Memory aids	78
	Index	86

1 Payment methods

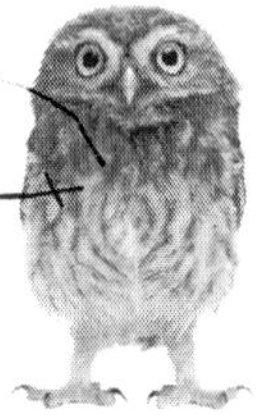

payment methods – old and new

There are many different ways of making payment, some centuries old and slow (eg the cheque) and some relatively new and much quicker (eg Faster Payments).

In your studies you will need to identify all the main types of payment and know which is most appropriate to each situation.

methods of payment

The main forms of making payment are:

- cash
- cheque
- debit card
- credit card
- BACS – direct credit and debit
- standing order
- Faster Payments
- CHAPS
- bank draft

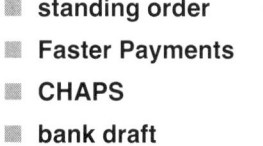

cash

Cash (notes and coins) is a traditional form of payment. Its use is declining as more people now use plastic cards. It is used in a number of situations:

- small purchases made by an organisation which operates a petty cash system, ie a store of cash kept under lock and key, normally within the Accounts Department
- cash wages – employees without a bank account who will need to be paid in cash through the Accounts Department

cheque

- a paper-based form of payment which has been in operation for over 350 years
- a cheque has to be paid in at a bank and sent to the bank of the person who issued it for payment (the issuer)
- if the cheque is in order (ie it is complete and has no errors or irregularities such as a missing signature) payment will be made to the bank of the person who has paid it in
- payment can be refused by the issuer's bank ('dishonoured') if there is not enough money in the issuer's account

debit card

- a plastic card used for making purchases at the counter, by telephone or online
- the money is taken out **electronically** from the purchaser's **bank account** normally within one or two days of the purchase, depending on the place or method of purchase

credit card

- a plastic card used for making purchases at the counter, by telephone or online
- the money is added on **electronically** to the purchaser's **credit card account**
- the customer pays the credit card company after the monthly statement arrives

standing order

- a bank-to-bank transfer set up by the person sending money
- the money is taken from the payer's bank account on the day of payment
- for regularly recurring payments (e.g. monthly) of same value
- used for: rent, loan repayments, subscriptions

BACS (Bankers Automated Clearing Services)

- a computer payment transfer system operated by the banks
- payment is set up electronically and is transferred electronically from bank account to bank account
- the clearing cycle is normally three days
- there are two main types of BACS transfer: direct credit and direct debit:

direct credits	direct debits
– regular bulk payments	– variable amounts
– variable amounts	– variable timing
– 3 day payment cycle	– 3 day payment cycle
– set up by business sending the money	– set up by business receiving the money
used for:	used for:
– paying wages	– power bills
– paying suppliers	– insurance premiums

Faster Payments

- a bank-to-bank **electronic** transfer system which enables customers to send payments to other bank accounts
- telephoned or online instructions accepted for immediate or future payments
- money transfer time **no more than two hours**
- intended for **small or medium-sized amounts**, maximum £250,000

CHAPS (Clearing House Automated Payments System)

- a bank-to-bank **electronic** transfer system
- **same day** irrevocable payments (ie payments cannot be cancelled)
- used for **high value** business-to-business payments, all types of property purchase

bank draft

- a **paper-based** transfer – a bank draft is a **bank cheque** (ie written out by a bank)
- a **high-value** transfer – guaranteed payment to the person receiving it
- used for **large purchases** where payment has to be guaranteed – eg car purchase

payment type	format	how it works
cheque	paper	sent to bank of issuer for payment, can be stopped
debit card	plastic	money deducted direct from customer's account
credit card	plastic	credit account settled monthly
standing order	electronic	set up by the person paying – fixed amounts and dates
BACS direct credit	electronic	bulk payments, eg payroll
BACS direct debit	electronic	set up by business being paid – variable amounts and dates
Faster Payments	electronic	set up by the person paying
CHAPS	electronic	very large payments
bank draft	paper	bank cheque – for large payments

2 Payment methods and the bank balance

payment methods – how they affect the bank balance

If a business is to manage its cash flow efficiently – in other words, the amount of money it has in the bank in order to pay its debts – it will need to keep unnecessary costs to a minimum.

The business will therefore have to avoid going overdrawn (ie having a negative balance on the bank account) more than it needs to.

the bank account – debit balances and credit balances

Before going any further it is important to note that a business and its bank will use the terms 'debit' and 'credit' when applied to the bank account in completely opposite ways. This can cause confusion, so the important thing is to remember the following rules:

cash book of a business	
debit =	money in the bank account
credit =	money owed to the bank (borrowing, eg overdraft)

bank statement	
debit =	money owed to the bank (borrowing, eg overdraft)
credit =	money in the bank account

the costs of running a business bank account

One reason for managing a bank account regularly and efficiently is to reduce the cost to the business of running the account (more costs = less profit). These costs include:

- bank charges for the day-to-day running of the account
- interest payable on overdrawn balances and any other borrowing
- 'arrangement' fees for setting up and renewing an overdraft or fixed loan

A business needs to minimise these account running costs. Good practice includes:

- keeping the account in credit (ie with a positive balance) whenever possible
- keeping overdrawn (debit) balances to a minimum
- paying money received into the bank account as soon as practically possible

On the next two pages you will see the different lengths of time it takes for different types of payment to be deducted from the bank account. Some payment systems take longer than others. The policy adopted by a business should be 'do not pay suppliers earlier than you have to, but do not pay after the due date – then you will breach the terms of supply and will upset the supplier'.

making payments – when is the money deducted from the account?

same day deduction	
cash withdrawal	the same day that the cash is withdrawn from the bank account
bank draft	the same day that the draft (the bank cheque) is issued to the customer by the bank
CHAPS	the same day that the payment is sent electronically to the recipient
Faster Payments	the electronic payment is normally received within two hours and includes standing orders

deduction later than the same day	
debit card	money normally deducted electronically direct from the payer's account one or two days later after payment is made
BACS direct credit	deducted from the account on the day that the recipient receives the money – the payment is set up three days in advance by business *making* the payment
BACS direct debit	deducted from the account on the day that the recipient receives the money – the payment is set up three days in advance by business *receiving* the payment
credit card	the monthly total of transactions is normally paid monthly
cheque	paper-based payment deducted from the issuer's account after the person to whom it is payable has received it and paid it into their own account – days or weeks later

3 Bank reconciliation statement

RECONCILING THE BANK STATEMENT AND CASH BOOK

A bank reconciliation statement sets out a calculation which explains the differences between a bank statement closing balance and the closing balance of the Bank account in the cash book. Bank reconciliation is a fiddly area to deal with and it is important to appreciate the effect of the differences that can occur.

where do you start?

One of the problems encountered is knowing where to start. A common method is to start with the bank statement closing balance and move towards the Bank account balance in the cash book. This is done by recording the adjustments in a bank reconciliation statement:

| Bank Statement | → | Bank Reconciliation Statement | → | Cash Book |

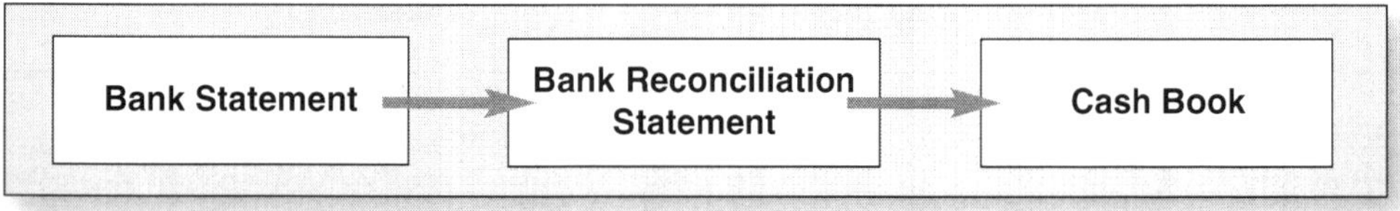

A summary of the calculation, with sample figures, looks like this:

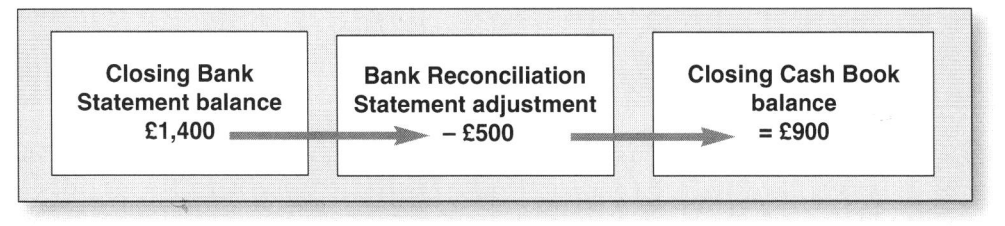

| Closing Bank Statement balance £1,400 | Bank Reconciliation Statement adjustment − £500 | Closing Cash Book balance = £900 |

the process for identifying differences

When you receive the bank statement you should carry out a ticking exercise which will identify any differences between the bank statement and the cash book entries.

- Tick off the items that are in the bank statement and also in the cash book bank columns. This will mean that you will most likely end up with unticked items in both the bank statement and the cash book.
- Update the cash book columns with the **unticked** items on the bank statement. These can include a variety of entries, eg bank charges and bank interest. You will need to be familiar with bank statements to know what the entries are. If in doubt, look at the bank statement on the next page and read the explanations that follow.

BANK STATEMENT					
Date	**Details**		**Paid out**	**Paid in**	**Balance**
20XX					
1 May	Balance				9,881.60
6 May	J Macmillan Ltd	BACS		561.60	10,443.20
10 May	683002	CHQ	115.44		10,327.76
13 May	AWA Finance	SO	360.00		9,967.76
17 May	Astley Insurance	DD	98.00		9,869.76
17 May	DoLittle & Dally	CHAPS	8,000.00		1,869.76

payment descriptions

BACS	computer transfer between bank accounts (**B**ankers **A**utomated **C**learing **S**ervices)
CHQ	**ch**e**q**ue (the cheque number is in the 'details' column)
SO	**S**tanding **O**rder — computer bank transfer set up by person paying the money
DD	**D**irect **D**ebit — computer bank transfer set up by business receiving money
CHAPS	Large amount same day bank computer transfer, often used by solicitors

updating the cash book entries

As you can see, there are a number of possible unticked items on a bank statement, all of which will need to be entered in the cash book. These are the main ones:

- BACS payments received from customers
- standing orders and direct debits paid out
- CHAPS payments out

Here are some other possibilities (not shown on the bank statement above):

- BACS payments sent to suppliers and BACS payments for wages
- bank charges and bank interest (paid or received)
- dishonoured (unpaid) cheques

closing cash book balance

When you have completed the update of the Bank account in the cash book, you should **balance the bank columns** to extract a final cash book balance.

This is the figure that will be inserted at the end of the Bank Reconciliation Statement.

dealing with the unticked items in the cash book

The differences that are now left between bank statement and cash book (assuming there are no errors) are the **unticked items in the cash book**. These are all **timing differences**:

unpresented cheques

These are cheques issued to suppliers or for other expenses; they have been written into the cash book but have not yet been deducted from the Bank account, and so are not on the bank statement.

outstanding lodgements

Receipts entered into the cash book but not yet recorded on the bank statement.

It is these items – the timing differences – which are entered into the Bank Reconciliation Statement to account for the difference between the final balances of the bank statement and updated cash book bank columns.

Study the sample bank reconciliation statement on the next page.

Bank Reconciliation Statement format

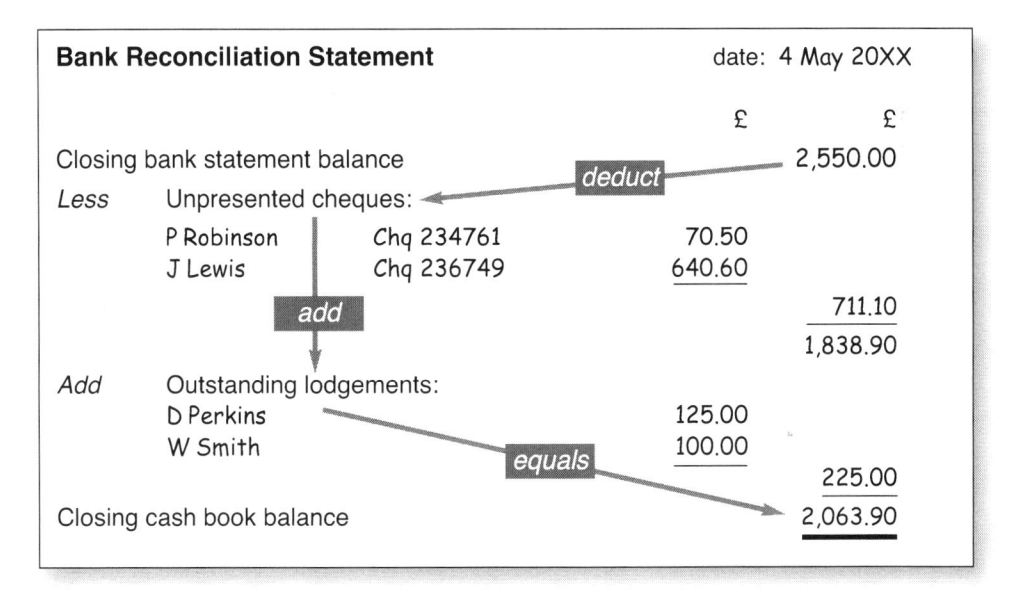

Bank Reconciliation Statement			date: 4 May 20XX
		£	£
Closing bank statement balance			2,550.00
Less Unpresented cheques:			
P Robinson	Chq 234761	70.50	
J Lewis	Chq 236749	640.60	
			711.10
			1,838.90
Add Outstanding lodgements:			
D Perkins		125.00	
W Smith		100.00	
			225.00
Closing cash book balance			**2,063.90**

Arrows in diagram: *deduct*, *add*, *equals*

principles of bookkeeping controls wise guide

the bank reconciliation process at a glance

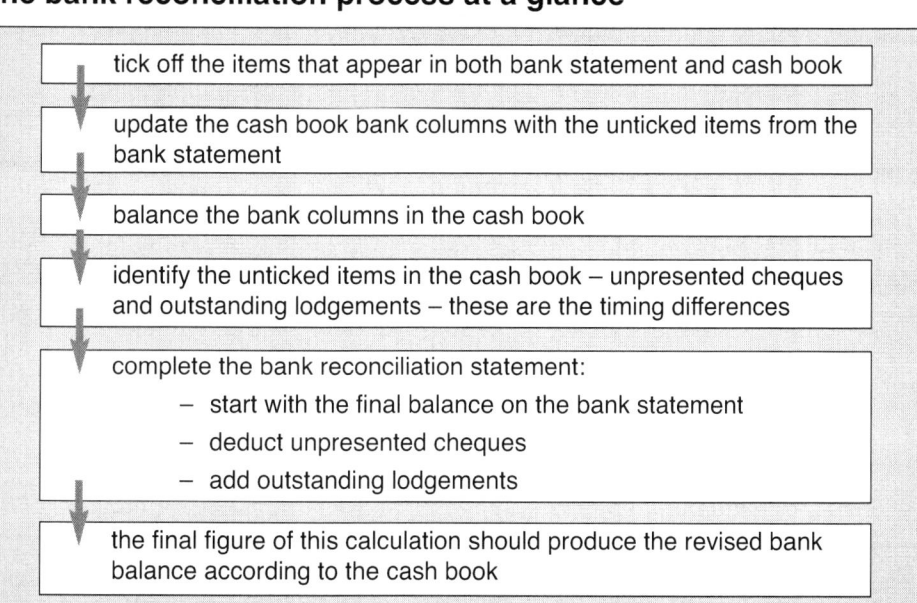

tick off the items that appear in both bank statement and cash book

update the cash book bank columns with the unticked items from the bank statement

balance the bank columns in the cash book

identify the unticked items in the cash book – unpresented cheques and outstanding lodgements – these are the timing differences

complete the bank reconciliation statement:

- start with the final balance on the bank statement
- deduct unpresented cheques
- add outstanding lodgements

the final figure of this calculation should produce the revised bank balance according to the cash book

summary of the completed bank reconciliation documents

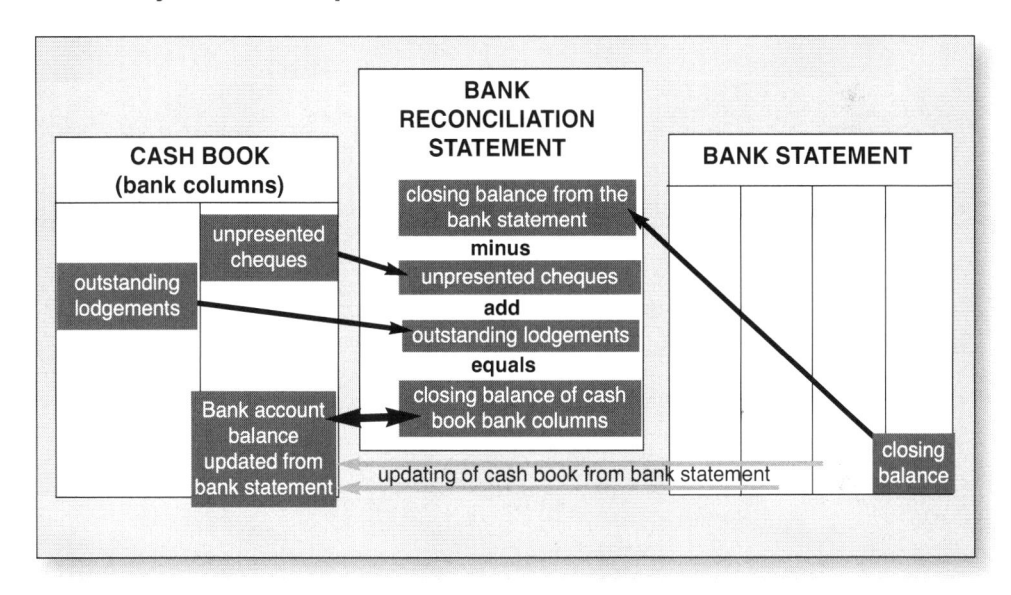

principles of bookkeeping controls wise guide

bank reconciliation complications

Watch out for

▨ Bank statement and cash book opening balances don't agree. Refer to the previous bank reconciliation, then look for unpresented and outstanding items at the beginning of the current period on the bank statement. Do not include these items in the current period bank reconciliation.

▨ The bank account may be overdrawn at the beginning of the period, or at the end, or both. The arithmetic is the same but use a negative number where the balance is overdrawn.

▨ The bank reconciliation statement format can start with the cash book balance and end with the bank statement balance. In this case the figures are: Balance per cash book, less outstanding items, add unpresented items = Balance per bank statement.

principles of bookkeeping controls wise guide

4 Receivables Ledger control account

Providing information about credit customers

When a business sells on credit to a customer, it is important that there is information about its customers (receivables) which shows how much is owed at any one time. It is also important that this information is correct.

*A **control account** is used both as a summary of this information and also as a checking device to make sure that the accounting system is accurate.*

what exactly is a control account?

- A control account is a 'master' account that provides information about a number of individual accounts, which are known as 'subsidiary' accounts.

- The **Receivables Ledger control account** is a 'master' account that controls individual 'subsidiary' accounts for each of its credit customers (receivables).

- The **Receivables Ledger control account** records the **totals** of different types of transactions – eg sales, sales returns, bank receipts – shown in the individual accounts.

Receivables Ledger control account as master account

Receivables Ledger Control Account	
totals of:	totals of:
Balances b/d	Bank (receipts)
Credit sales	Sales returns
Returned cheques	Discounts allowed
	Irrecoverable debts
	Balances c/d

RECEIVABLES LEDGER customer individual accounts

Atlas Limited

Balance b/d	Bank receipts
Sales	Sales returns
	Balance c/d

Bartro Limited

Balance b/d	Bank receipts
Sales	Sales returns
	Balance c/d

Celia Limited

Balance b/d	Bank receipts
Sales	Discounts all'wd
	Balance c/d

Delia Limited

Balance b/d	Irrecoverable
Sales	debts
Returned cheque	

Note about double-entry

Receivables Ledger control account is a double-entry account in the General Ledger. The entries in the customer Receivables Ledger subsidiary accounts **are not part of the double-entry system**.

The entries in the control account and the individual accounts are on the **same side**.

principles of bookkeeping controls wise guide

what are the entries in the Receivables Ledger control account?

Receivables Ledger Control Account			
Dr			**Cr**
Balance b/d	10,000	**Bank**	15,000
total customer balances brought down		*total receipts from credit customers*	
Credit sales	19,500	**Credit sales returns**	480
total credit sales to customers		*total sales returns from customers*	
Returned cheques	500	**Discounts allowed**	195
dishonoured (bounced) cheques issued by customers		*total discounts allowed to customers*	
		Irrecoverable debts	900
		total irrecoverable debts written off	
total customer balances at end of period		**Balance c/d**	13,425
	30,000		30,000
Balance b/d	13,425		

where in the accounting system do the entries come from?

Receivables Ledger Control Account				
Dr				**Cr**
Balance b/d	10,000		**Bank**	15,000
balance of the account brought down			*cash book receipts*	
Credit sales	19,500		**Credit sales returns**	480
sales day book total (including VAT)			*sales returns day book total (inc. VAT)*	
Returned cheques	500		**Discounts allowed**	195
cash book, credit side (cheques deducted by the bank)			*discounts allowed day book total column*	
			Irrecoverable debts	900
			irrecoverable debts written off account	
balance of account carried down		←	**Balance c/d**	13,425
	30,000			30,000
Balance b/d	13,425			

principles of bookkeeping controls wise guide

reconciling the control account with the individual accounts

Reconciling the Receivables Ledger control account is a useful way of checking the accuracy of the balances in the Receivables Ledger individual accounts.

The process is as follows (using the example on the previous page, with figures):

▓ The individual customer accounts are balanced at regular intervals. The balance b/d (brought down) in each case will be a **debit** in normal circumstances.

▓ The Receivables Ledger control account is balanced at the same time and the balance brought down on the **debit** side. The balance in this case is £13,425.

▓ The individual customer account balances are listed on a schedule and totalled:

BALANCES OF RECEIVABLES at 2 April 20XX	
Atlas Limited	£3,501
Bartro Limited	£6,030
Celia Limited	£3,894
Delia Limited	£0*
TOTAL	£13,425

- The customer accounts total and the Receivables Ledger control account balance agree. The figure is £13,425.
- There are no errors or discrepancies in the bookkeeping.

possible discrepancies in the reconciliation

When reconciling the total credit customer balances (receivables) with the Receivables Ledger control account final balance, you need to be aware of the types of discrepancy that can occur.

When faced with a difference, you will need to work out the amount of the difference and establish which total is the higher.

The differences can result from:

- wrong figures entered (too high or too low), eg total individual balances £7,418 entered as £7,148 in RLCA
- figures omitted, eg irrecoverable debt written off in individual account but not in RLCA
- figures entered twice, eg Discounts All'd entered twice in RLCA
- figures entered on the wrong side of an account, eg individual account credit balance treated as debit balance

managing customer accounts – irrecoverable debts

- A well run business will keep a careful eye on the balances of its customers in its Receivables Ledger.

- If any customer who buys on credit goes 'bust', the seller is likely to be left with a customer debt in its Receivables Ledger which it is unlikely to be able to recover. This is known as an **irrecoverable debt**.

- As an irrecoverable debt represents a loss to the business, it will have to be written off in the accounts and eventually deducted from profit:

  - debit **Irrecoverable debts expense account**
  - credit **Receivables Ledger control account** (and customer individual account)

5 Payables Ledger control account

Providing information about credit purchases

When a business buys on credit from suppliers (payables), it is important that the business knows how much is owed at any one time, and that it pays on time. It is very important that this information is accurate.

*A **control account** is used both as a summary of this information and also as a checking device to make sure that the accounting system is accurate.*

what exactly is a control account?

- A control account is a 'master' account that provides information about a number of individual accounts, which are known as 'subsidiary' accounts.

- The **Payables Ledger control account** is a 'master' account that 'controls' individual 'subsidiary' accounts for each of its suppliers (payables).

- The **Payables Ledger control account** records the **totals** of types of transaction – eg purchases, purchases returns, bank payments – shown in the individual accounts.

Payables Ledger control account as master account

Payables Ledger Control Account	
totals of:	**totals of:**
Bank (payments)	Balances b/d
Purchases returns	Credit purchases
Discounts received	
Balances c/d	

PAYABLES LEDGER supplier individual accounts

Allora Limited	
Bank payments	Balance b/d
Purchases returns	Purchases
Balance c/d	

Bella Limited	
Bank payments	Balance b/d
Purchases returns	Purchases
Balance c/d	

Centro Limited	
Bank payments	Balance b/d
Discounts received	Purchases
Balance c/d	

Dritto Limited	
Bank payments	Balance b/d
Purchases returns	Purchases
Balance c/d	

Note about double-entry

Payables Ledger control account is a double-entry account in the General Ledger. The entries in the supplier Payables Ledger individual accounts **are not part of the double-entry system**.

The entries in the control account and the individual accounts are on the **same side**.

principles of bookkeeping controls wise guide

what are the entries in the Payables Ledger control account?

Payables Ledger Control Account			
Dr			**Cr**
Bank	12,000	**Balance b/d**	14,000
total payments to credit suppliers		*total supplier balances brought down*	
Purchases returns	760	**Purchases**	18,000
total purchases returns to suppliers		*total credit purchases from suppliers*	
Discounts received	240		
total discounts received from suppliers			
Balance c/d	19,000	*total credit supplier balances at end of period*	
	32,000		32,000
		Balance b/d	19,000

where in the accounting system do the entries come from?

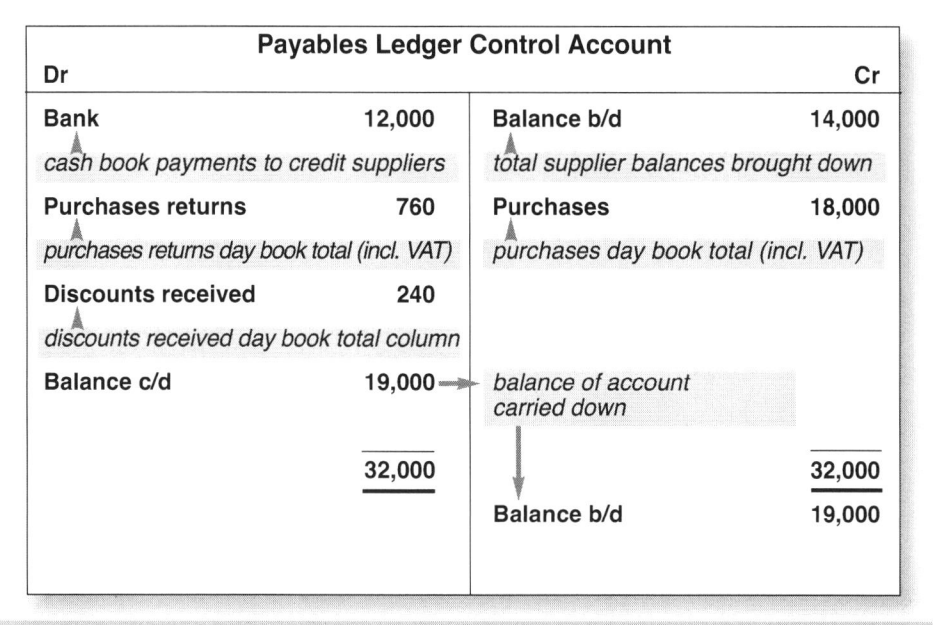

Payables Ledger Control Account			
Dr			**Cr**
Bank	12,000	Balance b/d	14,000
cash book payments to credit suppliers		*total supplier balances brought down*	
Purchases returns	760	Purchases	18,000
purchases returns day book total (incl. VAT)		*purchases day book total (incl. VAT)*	
Discounts received	240		
discounts received day book total column			
Balance c/d	19,000	*balance of account carried down*	
	32,000		32,000
		Balance b/d	19,000

reconciling the control account with the individual accounts

Reconciling the Payables Ledger control account is a useful way of checking the accuracy of the balances in the Payables Ledger individual accounts.

The process is as follows (using the example on the previous page, with figures):

■ The individual supplier accounts are balanced at regular intervals. The balance b/d (brought down) in each case will be a **credit** in normal circumstances.

■ The Payables Ledger control account is balanced at the same time and the balance brought down on the **credit** side. The balance in this case is £19,000.

■ The individual supplier account balances are listed on a schedule and totalled:

BALANCES OF PAYABLES at 2 April 20XX	
Allora Limited	£6,716
Bella Limited	£7,602
Centro Limited	£4,991
Dritto Limited	£309 (debit balance)
TOTAL	£19,000

- The supplier accounts total and the Payables Ledger control account balance agree. The figure is £19,000.
- There are no errors or discrepancies in the bookkeeping.

possible discrepancies in the reconciliation

When reconciling the total credit supplier balances (payables) with the Payables Ledger control account final balance, you need to be aware of the types of discrepancy that can occur.

When faced with a difference, you will need to work out the amount of the difference and establish which total is the higher.

The differences can result from:

- wrong figures entered (too high or too low), eg total of Purchase Returns £924 entered as £942 in PLCA
- figures omitted, eg journal entered in individual account but not in PLCA
- figures entered twice, eg Discount Rec'd entered twice in PLCA
- figures entered on the wrong side of an account, eg Discounts rec'd entered on credit side of PLCA

6 VAT control account

Collecting accounting data for the VAT Return

VAT is a tax on sales and an important money earner for the UK Government. All except the smallest businesses need to register for VAT.

A business needs to keep detailed and accurate accounting records and totals of VAT it pays on what it buys and VAT it charges on what it sells.

The difference between these two figures is the amount that has to be settled with HMRC.

A business will therefore need to complete a VAT Return on a regular basis to work out the amount it will either pay to – or claim back from – the tax office.

*A **VAT control account** collects all this information together and calculates the amount of VAT due. An example of the account format is shown on the next page.*

accounting records (books of prime entry)	→	**VAT CONTROL ACCOUNT** (General Ledger)	→	online VAT Return (VAT paid or claimed back online)

EXAMPLE: VAT Control Account

VAT Control Account

Dr			Cr
Purchases	20,000	Sales	30,000
Sales returns	2,800	Purchases returns	4,500
Discounts allowed day book	200	Discounts received day book	100
Cash purchases	5,000	Cash sales	6,400
Petty cash	16		
VAT on irrecoverable debts	124		
Balance c/d	12,860	VAT due to HMRC	
	41,000		41,000
		Balance b/d	12,860

- VAT paid by a business on its purchases can be claimed back from HMRC
- VAT charged by a business on its sales has to be paid to HMRC
- a credit balance b/d is the amount due to HMRC
- a debit balance b/d is the amount due from HMRC (a refund)

principles of bookkeeping controls wise guide

42

what are the debit entries in the VAT control account?

VAT Control Account extract (debit side)	
Purchases	20,000
Sales returns	2,800
Discounts allowed	200
Cash purchases	5,000
Petty cash	16
VAT on irrecoverable debts	124
Balance c/d	12,860
	41,000

Purchases Day Book, VAT column total – VAT paid on credit purchase invoices.

Sales Returns Day Book, VAT column total – VAT allowed on credit notes to customers.

Discounts Allowed Day Book VAT column total of prompt payment discount given.

Cash Book – VAT column total of VAT paid on cash purchases.

Petty Cash Book – VAT column total of VAT paid on petty cash purchases.

VAT previously paid to HMRC, now part of an **irrecoverable debt written off**. HMRC allows this VAT to be claimed back by the seller.

Balance carried down onto credit side of the account – **VAT due to be paid to HMRC**. It is a liability and so will be a credit balance.

What are the credit entries in the VAT control account?

Sales Day Book, VAT column total – VAT charged on credit sales invoices.

Purchases Returns Day Book, VAT column total – VAT on credit notes from suppliers.

Discounts Received Day Book – VAT column total of prompt payment discount.

Cash Book – VAT column total of VAT paid on cash sales.

Balance brought down on credit side of the account – **VAT due to be paid to HMRC**. It is a liability and therefore a credit balance.

If the balance had been brought down on the debit side, it would have been VAT owed by HMRC and therefore an asset.

VAT Control Account extract (credit side)	
Sales	30,000
Purchases returns	4,500
Discounts received	100
Cash sales	6,400
	41,000
Balance b/d	12,860

principles of bookkeeping controls wise guide 43

7 Journals – introduction

Books of prime entry – the role of the journal

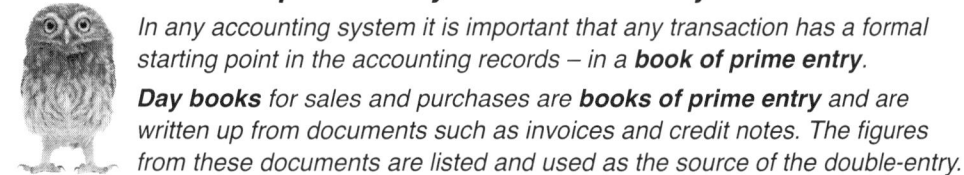

*In any accounting system it is important that any transaction has a formal starting point in the accounting records – in a **book of prime entry**.*

***Day books** for sales and purchases are **books of prime entry** and are written up from documents such as invoices and credit notes. The figures from these documents are listed and used as the source of the double-entry.*

*But there are other transactions which do not involve a formal document, eg an irrecoverable debt written off, an error in the accounts, notified by email. These will need to be recorded formally so that the double-entry can be carried out accurately and in an organised way. This is done in a **book of prime entry** called the **journal**.*

definition of the journal

- The journal is the book of prime entry for accounting transactions not catered for in the other routinely used books of prime entry, eg the day books.

- The journal lists transactions so that they can be entered in the double-entry accounts in the General Ledger.

use of the journal

- The journal can be used for transactions such as:
  - setting up the opening (first) entries in a set of accounts for a new business
  - writing off irrecoverable debts
  - writing up the double-entry accounts for payroll transactions (wages, salaries, tax)
  - correcting errors in the accounting system

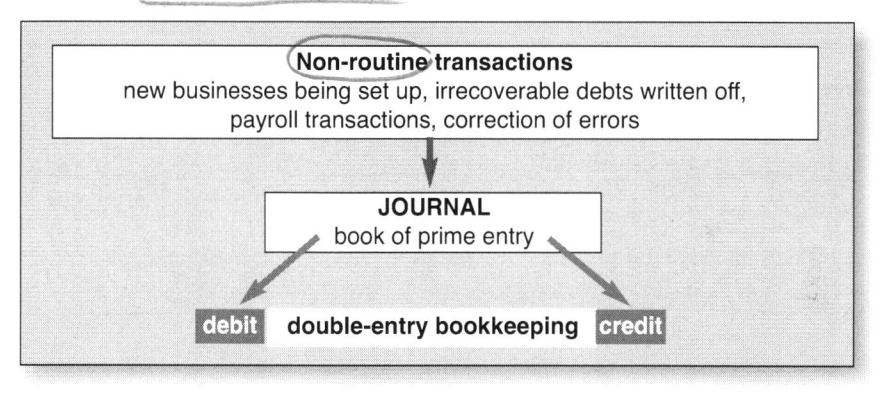

```
┌─────────────────────────────────────────────────────────────┐
│                   Non-routine transactions                   │
│   new businesses being set up, irrecoverable debts written off, │
│        payroll transactions, correction of errors            │
└─────────────────────────────────────────────────────────────┘
                              │
                              ▼
                    ┌──────────────────┐
                    │     JOURNAL      │
                    │ book of prime entry │
                    └──────────────────┘
                     ↙              ↘
            ┌───────┐                  ┌────────┐
            │ debit │ double-entry bookkeeping │ credit │
            └───────┘                  └────────┘
```

principles of bookkeeping controls wise guide

format of the journal

The journal format is set out as follows:

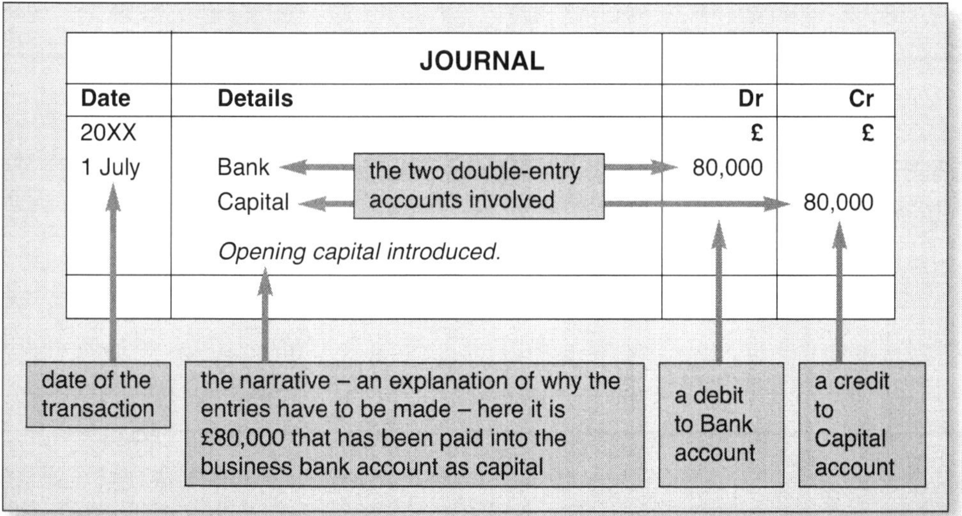

	JOURNAL		Dr	Cr
Date	Details		£	£
20XX				
1 July	Bank	the two double-entry accounts involved	80,000	
	Capital			80,000
	Opening capital introduced.			

date of the transaction → Date

the narrative – an explanation of why the entries have to be made – here it is £80,000 that has been paid into the business bank account as capital

a debit to Bank account

a credit to Capital account

notes on the format of the journal

- The account names are shown in the Details column and the debit entry is listed first.
- The narrative which follows the account names is the reason for the journal entry.
- There are columns for the required debit and credit entries.
- The debit column is to the left and the credit column is to the right.
- The debit and credit columns should always balance (ie have the same total).
- Each entry is ruled off at the bottom to separate it from the next entry.
- There may be more than two account entries in a transaction, but the debit and credit entries must always balance, as in this irrecoverable debt write off:

Date	Details	Dr	Cr
20XX		£	£
30 June	Irrecoverable debts expense	800.00	
	VAT	160.00	
	Receivables Ledger control		960.00
	Irrecoverable debt written off.	960.00	960.00

principles of bookkeeping controls wise guide

8 Journals – opening entries

Setting up a new accounting system

There will be times when a new accounting system will have to be set up from scratch, for example when a business starts up for the first time. In cases like these there are no existing double-entry accounts and the journal will be the book of prime entry to generate entries for the accounts.

It is quite possible that the business may have been trading already and there will be existing totals for sales and purchases and money in the bank to account for.

opening journal entries – debit or credit?

If you are opening up a set of accounts for the first time, you are likely to be faced with a list of figures for assets, liabilities, capital, VAT, purchases and sales, but with **no indication of whether they are debits or credits**. You will need to be able to work out which they are in order to enter your journal entries and get the debits and credits to balance. You should try to memorise the list on the next page.

debits	credits
Bank account (cash at bank)	Bank overdraft
Property	Capital
Vehicles	Bank loan
Expenses items	Income items
Purchases	Sales
VAT on purchases	VAT on sales
Receivables Ledger control account	Payables Ledger control account
TOTAL DEBITS ←— *equals* —→	TOTAL CREDITS

Debits =
- Assets
- Bank (cash in the bank)
- Purchases and expenses
- VAT on purchases
- Receivables Ledger control account

Credits =
- Liabilities and capital
- Bank overdraft and loans
- Sales and income
- VAT on sales
- Payables Ledger control account

50

EXAMPLE: Journal for opening entries

You have just started in business and have been trading for a month.

You have kept accurate accounting records but have not yet set up a double-entry system. Your accountant has suggested that you:

■ enter all the following amounts in a journal

■ make sure that the journal balances (ie the debit and credit totals agree)

■ set up the double-entry accounts

The amounts to enter are:

	£
Bank (cash at bank)	1,490
Purchases	10,500
Sales	12,000
Inventory	5,000
Computer equipment	12,500
Capital	17,490

The journal will look like this:

Date	Details	Dr	Cr
20XX		£	£
1 July	Bank (cash at bank)	1,490	
	Purchases	10,500	
	Inventory	5,000	
	Computer equipment	12,500	
	Sales		12,000
	Capital		17,490
		29,490	29,490
	Opening entries at start of business		

Note that:

- the debits are entered first and the credits last
- the total of the debits and the total of the credits agree
- double-entry accounts can now be set up and the debits and credits entered in them

principles of bookkeeping controls wise guide

9 Journals – irrecoverable debts

Writing off irrecoverable debts

*A business will sometimes encounter the situation where a customer debt becomes **irrecoverable** – in other words, despite all its efforts in trying to get the money back, the customer will not, or cannot, repay it.*

The debt will be recorded in the customer account in the Receivables Ledger and is likely also to include VAT charged to the customer. This will need to be 'written off' – ie taken out of the Receivables Ledger as a loss to the business.

the process of writing off an irrecoverable debt

The accounting entries needed are:

debit   Irrecoverable debts expense account

debit   VAT account

credit   Receivables Ledger control account (and the customer individual account)

This is set up by a **journal entry**, usually authorised by a managerial email (which will be attached to the journal as evidence of the transaction)

EXAMPLE: Apex Glazing's account written off as an irrecoverable debt

Date	Details	Dr	Cr
20XX		£	£
31 May	Irrecoverable debts expense	200	
	VAT	40	
	Receivables Ledger control		240
		240	240
	Balance of Apex Glazing's Receivables Ledger account written off as an irrecoverable debt, authorised by email from S Tingi, Accounts Manager.		

Note that:

- the debt of £240 is split into the sales amount (£200) and the VAT (£40)
- the debits come before the credit and the totals balance
- the narrative quotes the email authorisation for the transaction

principles of bookkeeping controls wise guide

10 Journals – payroll transactions

processing the payroll

Processing the payroll is a complicated procedure. The employer has to pay the employees and also needs to calculate and make all the deductions for tax, National Insurance Contributions, pension contributions and voluntary deductions to various bodies.

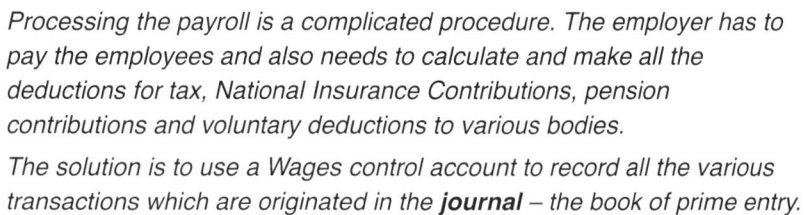

*The solution is to use a Wages control account to record all the various transactions which are originated in the **journal** – the book of prime entry.*

what are the transactions?

The payments you need to remember are listed here and on the next page – they should be memorised:

▨ **gross pay** – the amount of pay before any deductions, eg tax, are made

▨ **net pay** – the amount which employees actually receive after deductions

- **Income tax** – the amount of tax deducted from employees' gross pay and paid to HMRC
- **National Insurance Contributions** – there are two amounts which the employer has to pay direct to HMRC:
  - the **employer's** National Insurance Contributions (NIC), an expense to the employer
  - the **employees'** National Insurance Contributions (NIC) deducted from employees' gross pay by the employer
- **Pension Contributions** – there are often two amounts which the employer has to pay direct to the pension provider:
  - the **employer's** pension contributions, ie pension contributions for the employees provided by the employer
  - the **employees'** pension contributions, deducted from employees' pay by the employer
- **Voluntary deductions** – amounts deducted from pay by the employer at the employee's request, eg Trade Union subscriptions, charitable donations

This is all illustrated in the diagram on the next page.

the payroll system – how payments are made by the employer

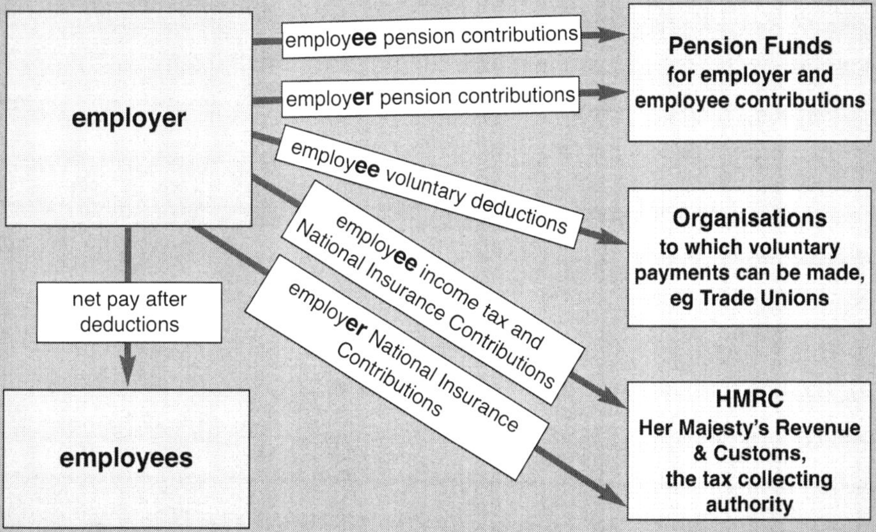

employer

employ**ee** pension contributions →

employ**er** pension contributions →

Pension Funds
for employer and
employee contributions

employ**ee** voluntary deductions →

Organisations
to which voluntary
payments can be made,
eg Trade Unions

employ**ee** income tax and
National Insurance Contributions →

employ**er** National Insurance
Contributions →

HMRC
Her Majesty's Revenue
& Customs,
the tax collecting
authority

net pay after
deductions ↓

employees

Wages control account

- All accounting entries relating to payroll pass through the **Wages control account**, which is written up from entries in the journal.
- The Wages control account is a proper double-entry account: a debit or credit to Wages control account will be a credit or debit in one of the other payroll accounts.

what do the other payroll accounts record?

- **Bank**
  - payment of net pay to employees
  - payments to HMRC of tax and National Insurance Contributions, pension contributions, voluntary deductions
- **Wages expense**
  - the payroll expense to the employer, ie . . .
  - employees' gross pay
  - employer's National Insurance Contributions (NIC)
  - any employer's pension or other contributions
- **HM Revenue & Customs**
  - amounts due to HM Revenue & Customs for income tax and National Insurance Contributions (NIC)
- **Pension funds**
  - contributions from both employer and employees

principles of bookkeeping controls wise guide

EXAMPLE: Wages Control Account

Wages Control Account			
Dr			**Cr**
Bank	26,000	Wages expense	39,910
HM Revenue & Customs	10,000		
Pension fund	3,670	these totals will equal each other, leaving a nil balance, and no balance to bring down	
Trade Union subscriptions	240		
	39,910		39,910

Note that normal double-entry rules apply to Wages control account:

- All debit entries in the **Wages control account** will require a credit entry in the 'other' account, for example a credit of £26,000 to Bank account for the wages paid.

- All credit entries in the **Wages control account** will require a debit entry in the 'other' account, for example a debit of £39,910 to Wages expense account.

how the journal fits into the payroll process

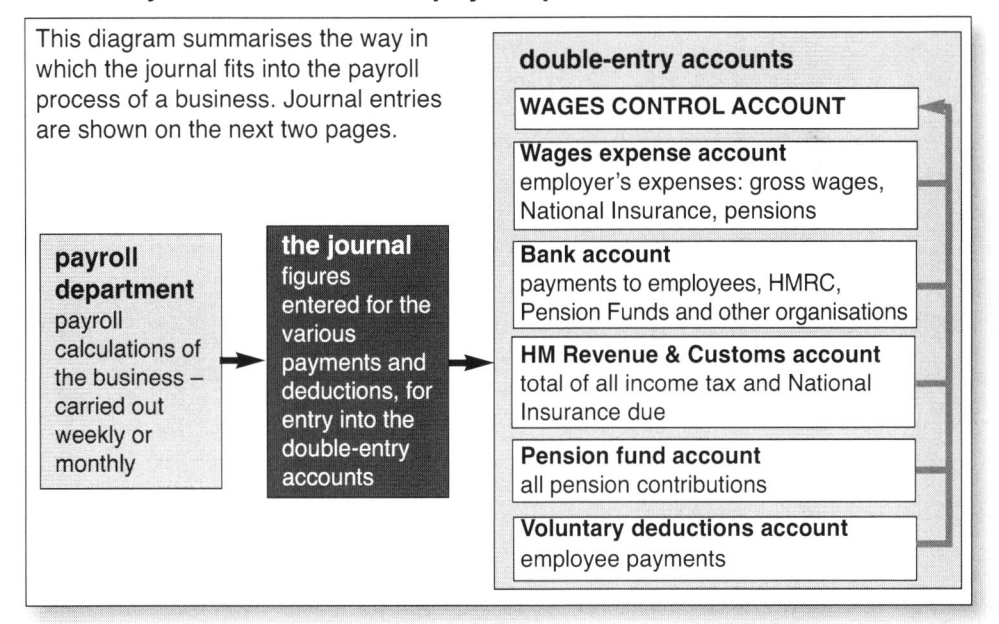

This diagram summarises the way in which the journal fits into the payroll process of a business. Journal entries are shown on the next two pages.

payroll department
payroll calculations of the business – carried out weekly or monthly

→

the journal
figures entered for the various payments and deductions, for entry into the double-entry accounts

→

double-entry accounts

WAGES CONTROL ACCOUNT

Wages expense account
employer's expenses: gross wages, National Insurance, pensions

Bank account
payments to employees, HMRC, Pension Funds and other organisations

HM Revenue & Customs account
total of all income tax and National Insurance due

Pension fund account
all pension contributions

Voluntary deductions account
employee payments

journal entries needed for processing payroll

These are the journal entries for the Wages control account on page 58. Note that:

▨ Each journal entry involves an entry in Wages control account.

▨ The 'other' account entry follows double-entry rules, for example Wages expense is a debit (an expense) and the other accounts are credits – bank payment and liabilities amounts owed.

Date	Details	Dr	Cr
20XX		£	£
30 June	Wages expense	39,910	
	Wages control		39,910
	transfer of wages expense		

Date	Details	Dr	Cr
20XX		£	£
30 June	Wages control	26,000	
	Bank		26,000
	net wages paid to employees		

Date	Details	Dr	Cr
20XX		£	£
30 June	Wages control	10,000	
	HM Revenue & Customs		10,000
	amount due to HM Revenue & Customs		

Date	Details	Dr	Cr
20XX		£	£
30 June	Wages control	3,670	
	Pension fund		3,670
	amount due to Pension fund		

Date	Details	Dr	Cr
20XX		£	£
30 June	Wages control	240	
	Trade Union fees		240
	amount due for Trade Union subscriptions		

11 Extracting an initial Trial Balance

*Double-entry always requires debits to equal credits. This can be checked by adding up all the debit balances and all the credit balances in the general ledger and **making sure the two totals are the same**.*

*This is known as the **Trial Balance**.*

the Trial Balance

- lists all the general ledger account balances at a specific date (eg the last day in the month) in two columns and adds them both up

- the left-hand column contains the debit balances and the right-hand column contains the credit balances

- the two totals *should* agree

EXAMPLE: TRIAL BALANCE

In the example here, a simple Trial Balance for ABC Ltd is drawn up on 31 May from the account balances shown on the left.

Account name	Balance (£)	ABC LTD TRIAL BALANCE AS AT 31 MAY Debit (£)	Credit (£)
Bank (cash at bank)	2,000	2,000	
Capital	20,000		20,000
Electricity	395	395	
Insurance	935	935	
Machinery	4,900	4,900	
Payables	2,700		2,700
Purchases	49,970	49,970	
Receivables	3,500	3,500	
Sales	81,000		81,000
VAT (payable to HMRC)	870		870
Wages	42,870	42,870	
		Total 104,570	104,570

principles of bookkeeping controls wise guide

debit or credit?

■ It helps to know which balances are debits and which are credits.

■ The rules are straightforward and can be remembered by the two words:

DEAD (for the **debits**)   **CLIC** (for the **credits**)

These words stand for the types of account listed in the Trial Balance:

D ebit balances	**C** redit balances
E xpenses	**L** iabilities
A ssets	**I** ncome
D rawings	**C** apital

'DEAD CLIC' is just one way of helping you to remember your debits and credits. Your tutor may suggest other ways. See Section 14 (page 78) for making your own 'Memory aids'.

notes on DEAD CLIC

DEAD = debit balances
Debits are items that a business owns, money it is owed and money it pays out.

- **D**ebits:
- **E**xpenses — Expenses of the business, eg purchases, wages, insurance.
- **A**ssets — Items owned by the business, eg money in bank, inventory, computers, property, receivables (amounts owed to the business).
- **D**rawings — Money or inventory taken out of a business by the owner(s).

CLIC = credit balances
Credits are items that a business owes and money it receives.

- **C**redits:
- **L**iabilities — Items owed by the business, eg loans, bank overdraft, payables (money owed to suppliers).
- **I**ncome — Money coming into the business, eg sales, rent received.
- **C**apital — Money invested by the owner in the business.

Trial Balance – points to watch out for

Nothing is ever completely straightforward in accounting and there are **some accounts which can have either debit or credit balances**.

These need to be transferred to either the debit or the credit column of the Trial Balance as appropriate.

You will always be given information which will tell you whether the balance is debit or credit.

There are two main examples:

Bank account	Money in the bank (sometimes called '**cash at bank**') is an **asset** and so will always be a **debit**.
	Money owed to the bank, eg a **bank loan** or an **overdraft**, is a **liability** and so will always be a **credit**.
VAT account	VAT account records Value Added Tax due to, or due from, HMRC (HM Revenue & Customs), ie the tax authorities.
	VAT **due to HMRC** = a **credit** balance
	VAT **due from HMRC** = a **debit** balance

some other debits and credits to remember . . .

Here are some other debit and credit account balances which you will need to remember. They all follow the basic DEAD CLIC rules for debits and credits.

Account name	Debit (£)	Credit (£)	Comment
Discounts allowed	XXXX		a decrease in sales income = an expense
Discounts received		XXXX	reduces cost of purchases = income
Purchases	XXXX		purchases = an expense
Payables ledger control		XXXX	total of supplier accounts = a liability
Sales		XXXX	sales = an income item
Receivables ledger control	XXXX		total of customer accounts = an asset (items owed to the business)

12 Journals – correction of errors and suspense account

sorting out accounting errors

One of the functions of a Trial Balance is to highlight any errors which might have occurred in the double-entry accounting system. If a Trial Balance does not balance, the difference will need to be calculated, located and corrected.

*A **suspense account** will be created and the difference entered in it. Entries will then be made in the suspense account to correct the errors, reducing its balance to zero.*

*All these correcting transactions will be originated using the **journal**.*

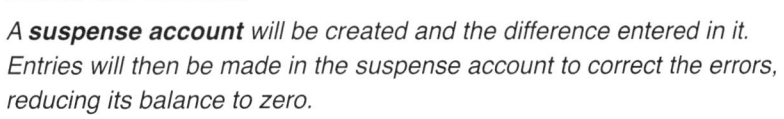

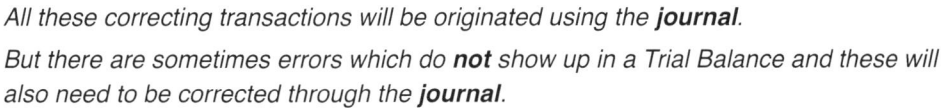

*But there are sometimes errors which do **not** show up in a Trial Balance and these will also need to be corrected through the **journal**.*

So, when dealing with errors the important thing you have to do is to decide if it is:

- *an error **not revealed** by the Trial Balance – no suspense account needed*

- *an error **revealed** by the Trial Balance – you will need a suspense account*

setting up the suspense account

- If the Trial Balance totals show a difference, **calculate** the difference, eg £300.
- Identify **which side** – debit or credit – has the higher total.
- If the **credit** side of the Trial Balance has the higher total, enter the figure on the **debit** side of suspense account . . .

Dr	Suspense account (credit side of Trial Balance greater)				Cr
		£			£
31 Dec	Trial Balance difference	300			

- If the **debit** side of the Trial Balance has the higher total, enter the figure on the **credit** side of suspense account . . .

Dr	Suspense account (debit side of Trial Balance greater)				Cr
		£			£
			31 Dec	Trial Balance difference	300

six errors not revealed by the Trial Balance (no suspense account)

- **error of omission** – a transaction has not been entered at all

- **error of commission** – a transaction has been entered in the wrong person's account, eg the wrong customer has been invoiced

- **error of principle** – a transaction has been entered in the wrong type of account, eg fuel for a vehicle has been entered in the vehicles account (an asset account) instead of in the fuel expense account

- **error of original entry** – a transaction has been entered using the same figure as both debit and credit, but using the wrong figure

- **reversal of entries** – the same figure has been entered but on the wrong side of both accounts involved

- **compensating error** – two separate errors cancel each other out, for example:
  - an overstatement **and** understatement of £50 on the same side, or
  - positive or negative errors on both sides, eg + £50 **or** – £50 on both sides

These errors may occur in both manual and digital systems.

six errors revealed by the Trial Balance (suspense account needed)

If the balances of the debit and credit columns of the Trial Balance do not agree, you should set up a suspense account with the difference – on the correct side. You will then use that figure and look for the error. It could be caused by any of the following:

- **calculation errors in accounts** – eg an error when adding up figures and balancing a ledger account

- **single entry transactions** – eg entering a debit but forgetting to enter the credit

- **using two debits or two credits** – eg debiting Insurance account and also debiting Bank account (which should have had a credit entry)

- **using different amounts on the debits and credits** – eg reversing figures such as £23 (debit) and £32 (credit)

- **error in transferring account balance to the Trial Balance** – simply entering a wrong figure in the Trial Balance, eg entering a balance of £5,500 instead of £5,550

- **omitting a General Ledger account in the Trial Balance** – leaving an account balance out of the Trial Balance completely

EXAMPLES: journals for correction of errors

error of omission not revealed on Trial Balance

Credit purchase of £480 including VAT on invoice 28374 from J R Supplies omitted from the accounting system. Invoice located having slipped behind filing cabinet.

The journal is the book of prime entry for entering the transaction into the accounting system.

Date	Details	Dr	Cr
20XX		£	£
30 June	Purchases	400.00	
	VAT	80.00	
	Payables Ledger control		480.00
		480.00	480.00
	Invoice 28374 omitted from accounts.		
	Payables Ledger: credit J R Supplies		

Note: a credit entry for £480 would be made in J R Supplies' Payables Ledger individual account.

EXAMPLE: error of principle not revealed on Trial Balance

The cost of property maintenance, £245 (no VAT), cash receipt 452, was debited to Property account (asset account) instead of Property maintenance account (expense account).

The journal (a book of prime entry) sets up the transfer of the £245 from Property account to Property maintenance account.

The credit to Property account cancels out the original incorrect debit for the same amount.

Date	Details	Dr	Cr
20XX		£	£
30 June	Property maintenance account	245.00	
	Property account		245.00
	Correction of error, receipt 452		

EXAMPLE: calculation error revealed by the Trial Balance

*The Trial Balance does not balance; the debit side is £50 higher than the credit side. There has been a calculation error of £50 in the Sales account which is £50 lower than it should be. £50 has been entered as a **credit** to Suspense account.*

You will need to cancel out the error and remove the £50 from the Suspense account. The journal entry is as follows:

Date	Details	Dr	Cr
20XX		£	£
30 June	Suspense	50.00	
	Sales		50.00
	Correction of undercasting of sales by £50		

double-entry needed:

Debit   **Suspense account** £50 (this entry cancels out the original credit for £50 and brings Suspense account to a zero balance).

Credit   **Sales account** £50 (this entry increases the balance of Sales account by £50 and brings it up to the correct balance).

EXAMPLE: single entry error revealed by the Trial Balance

*The Trial Balance does not balance: the **credit side** total is £150 **higher** than the debit side total. A cash purchase for £150 (no VAT) has been made but not recorded in Cash purchases account. In order to get the Trial Balance to balance, £150 is **debited** to Suspense account.*

*You will need to correct the error by **debiting** Cash purchases account £150 and **crediting** Suspense account £150. The journal entry is as follows:*

Date	Details	Dr	Cr
20XX		£	£
30 June	Cash purchases	150.00	
	Suspense		150.00
	Correction of error – omission of entry to		
	Cash purchases account		

double-entry needed:

Debit **Cash purchases account** £150 to correct the omission

Credit **Suspense account** £150 to bring the account balance to zero

13 Redrafting the Trial Balance

correcting the Trial Balance

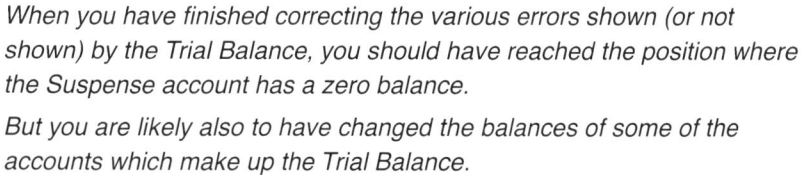

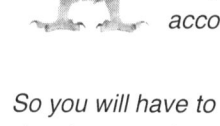

When you have finished correcting the various errors shown (or not shown) by the Trial Balance, you should have reached the position where the Suspense account has a zero balance.

But you are likely also to have changed the balances of some of the accounts which make up the Trial Balance.

*So you will have to **redraft the Trial Balance** and total the columns again, with the result that the total of the debit balances should now equal the total of the credit balances.*

Redrafting the Trial Balance and adjustments

- Recalculate the balance of any General Ledger account that has changed.
- Complete the Trial Balance using adjusted and unadjusted balances.
- Check that the totals of the debit and credit columns match.

14 Memory aids

KEEPING YOUR MEMORY FIT

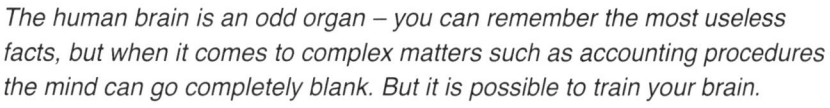

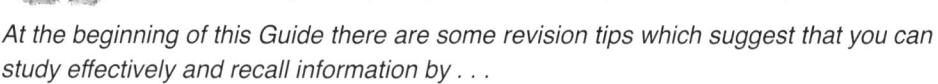

The human brain is an odd organ – you can remember the most useless facts, but when it comes to complex matters such as accounting procedures the mind can go completely blank. But it is possible to train your brain.

At the beginning of this Guide there are some revision tips which suggest that you can study effectively and recall information by . . .

- ■ ***Observing***, *ie remembering what information looks like on the page, using diagrams, lists, mind-maps and colour coding. Memory is very visual.*

- ■ ***Writing*** *information down, using flash cards, post-it notes, notes on a phone. It is the actual process of writing which helps to fix the information in the brain.*

- ■ ***Learning*** *by regularly going through your course notes and text books. Find a 'study buddy' in your class (or online) to teach and test each other as the course progresses.*

- **Chill out** when you get tired. Give your brain a chance to recover. Get some exercise and fresh air, work out. In the ancient world there was the saying that "a fit body is home to a fit mind".

- **Treats** – promise yourself rewards when you have finished studying – meet friends, eat chocolate, have a drink, listen to music.

exam preparation

- **Practise, practise, practise** when preparing for your assessment.

  Practise the questions and assessments in the Osborne Books workbooks.

some aids to memory

Write the names of the accounts on the correct sides of the control account.

debits	RECEIVABLES LEDGER CONTROL ACCOUNT	credits
bal b/d	Dis allowed	
Sales invoice		

debits	PAYABLES LEDGER CONTROL ACCOUNT	credits
Dis received		bal b/d
		purch invoice

82

Write the names of the accounts on the correct sides of the VAT account.

debits	VAT CONTROL ACCOUNT	credits

Write the names of the accounts on the correct sides of the Wages control account.

debits	**WAGES CONTROL ACCOUNT**	credits

On the next two pages are blank spaces for you to set out ways of remembering debit and credit entries. Please note that if you wish to use word prompts such as 'DEAD CLIC' **make sure first** that you understand **why** each entry goes on a particular side.

1   **Double-entry** – on which side does the entry go? Make a list on the T account format below of what type of accounts are normally debits and which are normally credits, eg purchases, sales, liabilities, assets, capital, drawings etc, etc . . .

debits	credits

Trial Balance – write out in the columns below some typical accounts found on a Trial Balance of a business (no figures needed). Make sure that you include in your list a bank loan, cash at bank and VAT due to HMRC . . .

debits	credits

Index

BACS, 9
Bank account, 12-15
    business bank account, 13
    costs, 13
    payment periods, 14-15
Bank draft, 10
Bank reconciliation statement, 16-24
Bank statement, 18

Cash, 7
CHAPS, 10
Cheques, 7
Correction of errors, 45,68-75
Credit card, 8

Debit card, 8
Direct credits, 9
Direct debits, 9
Dishonoured cheques, 7

Errors
    not revealed by the Trial Balance, 70
    revealed by the Trial Balance, 71

Faster Payments, 10

Irrecoverable debts, 32

Journals
- correction of errors, 68
- format, 46-47
- introduction, 44-45
- irrecoverable debts, 52-53
- opening entries, 48-51
- payroll transactions, 54-61

Outstanding lodgements, 20-23

Payment methods, 6-11
Payroll, 54-61
Payables Ledger control account, 34-39
- entries, 36-37
- individual accounts, 35
- reconciliation, 38-39

Receivables Ledger control account, 26-33
- entries, 28-29
- individual accounts, 27
- reconciliation, 30-31

Standing orders, 8
Suspense account, 68,69,71

Trial Balance 62-77
- extracting, 62-67
- redrafting, 76

Unpresented cheques, 20-23

VAT control account, 40-43
- entries, 42-43

Wages control account, 54,57-61